VIA Folios 173

The Birthday Years

(From 1947 to 2023)

Rachel Guido deVries

The Birthday Years

(From 1947 to 2023)

Library of Congress Control Number: 2024942218

Published by
Bordighera Press
John D. Calandra Italian American Institute
25 W. 43rd Street, 17th Floor
New York, NY 10036

VIA Folios 173
ISBN 978-1-59954-221-8

Contents

For
Marietta Guido Rappise
and Josephine Guido Puglis
in gratitude

Author's Note

I have been writing poems for my own birthday off and on since I was eleven years old. Now approaching seventy-six, I have put the poems and reflections together, and I think they tell my story. I also like seeing my own work grow and change with the passing of years. A few years are missing, and I am not sure why. Some birthdays, I wrote more than one poem, and some years I included poems written a month or so before or after September 9th to offer a sense of my life at those times. I have kept a journal off and on, mostly on, since I was ten years old. The last poem was written for my seventy-fifth birthday, 9 September 2022. This was an incredibly sad birthday—two dear friends, and mother and daughter—were killed by a drugged driver in August, 2022. My last (so far!) birthday poem is a sad one. So I included 'Purple' to ring back to the beginning poem and see the 'purple' coloring it's way through the poems.

Deborah Sorrentino was a fine poet, and an avid reader. We were often on the phone, sharing poems, ideas for poems and books to read. I miss her beautiful and powerful poems, and I especially miss talking books with her. I miss her bawdy laughter and her mischievous sense of humor. Her mother, Pat, was at ninety-three beautiful and both Pat and Deborah were full of life, love, and joy. I hope all who knew each of them carry that legacy forward.

Some of these poems previously appeared in *Voices in Italian Americana*, *The Paterson Literary Review*, and in *How to Sing to a Dago* (Guernica, 1996).

Dear Diary

Today is my birthday.
I had lots of fun.
We had a hula hoop contest
and Anna Mae Meyer won.

The prize
was a purple hula hoop.
She liked it very much
because
she didn't have one.

1958
Eleven years old

Birthday Tomato
A Memory from When I Was Twelve

back there, eating a jersey tomato with mamma on the steps, early
evening and the air was cool. all day it had been hot and muggy, a
real northern new jersey end-of-summer day, and in a couple of
weeks the hurricanes would start, and mamma would make us all run
out under the crackling wires and into the swirling rain until mr.
perrotti yelled at her from the window to get us all back in before we
were electrocuted.

i love to remember that and how we must have looked, me and rita,
and little johnny. i was twelve, rita nine and johnny was about two
and a half. he toddled out into the street on his own, mamma frantic,
and waving her arms, like she was trying to be a traffic cop to the
storm. later, we all laughed, and we still laugh about it today, decades
later, but little Johnny is gone and so is pop, both of them now like
the clouds, sometimes placid and always full of some emotion about
to bust out of the clouds into life.

but outside with mamma on my birthday, tomato juice running
down our chins, we counted cars to marriage, matched the color of
a car to the eyes of an imagined boyfriend, even though mamma
always knew who she would love. his black eyes like the chevy impala
he drove, smoky and wondering, off in his car right now and looking

her black hair lifting gently in a breeze, eyes
shut behind secrets, trapped in a cave of sorrow.
An echo sways sometimes through slits in gray walls,
the key blue as ocean waves humming and it is this
she learns all her life to listen for, a sound

shimmering on stone in her open palm

Poem at Twenty-Two

Before Marriage

I wonder.
Today I am twenty-two
and our lives
mine and his
are soon to merge.

We have dreams and hopes
We are idealistic
and sometimes realistic.

We are young and strong
but frightened and weak.
I wonder how we will be.

To fall into emptiness around us
To emulate the untogether marriages of some
would ruin us both.
I pray we will remain aware of us
and work to have 'us'
with us
always.

Twenty-Third Year

Twenty-three today
My first birthday with love
Here
our new home
new places to be
we find our way
slowly
but strongly
and mostly together

Love is full
and daily we play
I love seeing him so close
and so in need of us
At times
I get scared

Twenty-three at times
seems like the aging process has begun
Sounds like it, I mean.
I feel no older than twenty.
But I don't want time
to sneak up and surprise my years
with aging.
Staying young
is for us.

Twenty-Seven: Mwaembe, Kenya

My birthday.
Twenty-seven years have passed within me.
Today, I celebrate at Mwaembe,
up at 6 a.m. watching the sunrise,
thinking about Erica Jong's poem
'Aging Balm for a Twenty-seventh Birthday'.

Morning unfolds and gently wraps itself
around me. I sit at my window
as the morning sun rises
and think of a woman I've begun to love.

The Indian Ocean rolls softly today.
Roosters crow.
Today, the children of my village
have returned to school.
It is quieter than usual,
and as usual, it is beautiful.

Is twenty-seven significant?
Just a number
affixed to the passing of time?
Here the Digo women rarely know their ages
and go on living, loving each day, week, month, and year.

I reach across miles and spaces
to call up new love and the place within me
that yearns for tenderness.

1974

To Scratch an Itch

In Kenya, the elephants
scratch themselves on rough bark
of baobob trees. Their hides
strip the trees bare; the itches bleat
unsoothed. Trees turn to nakedness.
A myth has devils lurking
in their very roots.

Here, I grovel for ways to calm
the motion of my restless blood.
I rub against lovers.
My nakedness is shameless.
The itch continues.

The bark of every tree is bare.
Devils invade my toes.

1974

The Ngong Hills, Kenya

Deep in the hills
my thirst yelled. We feared
buffalo hidden around bends.
What mattered most was a brief pause
when we spoke of infinity.
There on the hills it all seemed
possible. When we met a Kikuyu woman
we spoke to her in Swahili, 'Shikamoo, Mama.
Habari gani asubuhi?'* 'Nzuri tu, Mzee.'*
She carried a calabash of water on her head.

My body thirsted. It breathed shallow.
The oxygen thinned high on the hills
and the faint I felt was not an illusion.
She offered me a cup of her water.

Closer to the sky than I'd ever been
I sought a split in the clouds, some
encouraging light cast down
from some ethereal god. What
I mostly wanted was to shore up
my resources, to hustle back to the life
I thought I knew. I spoke of the only thing
I was sure of. This body, as firm as its flesh

1974

*Greetings: *Shikamoo* is a term of respect. How are you this morning.
Her reply: 'Only good, Sir.'

Spoken from the Calabash

Can be sounds of fear,
turbulent, moving in a spiral,
a dream state when the body immobilizes.
Mothers, friends, beckon, appear
sinister and misshapen.

It takes days to survive
remembering, remembering, and urging
the present clean. Backyard journeys
clutter like an ache on the will,
sad for itself, nostalgia for a world
I can't live in.

Forward, backward, around and around,
little wings, the tiny bird
near my heart, the fluttering
triumphs of flight. The rest
the heart needs to discover.

In a moment I could turn to the sea,
float there or uncover a mystery,
a dream of the universe.

Gulls call. This is today.

Shimoni, Kenya, 1974

20

*

A feeling all in colors. The drawing
comes like a poem, perfect eyes, lips
find themselves in something known, so old,
like the flute's perfect pitch at sunrise.
This is the color, the sound, a landing site
to live for.

*

Sometimes I hear voices. I listen.
They say, 'Turn left.'
They say, 'The heart the mirror the eyes.'

*

There were four spirits in the calabash
in Shimoni, in Kenya. Three were out walking.
I had to wait for their return,
pay respect, and listen, I heard soft voices.
I was *kali*, they said,
Fierce.
Kali sana.
Very fierce,
and oh yes, I trembled.

Kali the will the hunger is keen
Kali sana as tree stretches to sky
and roots so deeply in earth

*

I land for days in the world. Get drunk,
make love. Everything lives in the body then,
everything becomes not real as the spinning dreams
and the knowledge they bring.
The imagination the body knows
better than lust or the soft inside of a woman.

*

It is me. Me. The hunger, the edge
of morning's delicate mouth, pink
and seductive. The light of candle
in day. The texture of sand. The life in parts
the way I fall in love part by part, and say the oh
of bliss, round and pliant.

*

I awaken to harmonies
to women full of spirits.
Kali   we are fierce
Kali sana   we are so fierce
spoken from the calabash.
The women are singing
filling the sky,
with our fierce songs of life.

Turning Thirty

cartwheels on the lawn
the feel of the grass
damp and soft like
a baby's tongue
in the small of my back
comes a shiver   a marble
of a feeling   shaded
in the darks and lights
the wet and dry
of changing age.
Here at this familiar desk
I read backwards through my journals
whizzing through my twenties
on retreads   some emotions
recycled worth saving
a stock pile   an arsenal
skills acquired   forgotten
remembered again
Always under my pillow
is a small stone of a tooth
one of thirty-two good ones
waiting for wishes for
fairies for an approaching
magic

1977

9 September 1987

Mamma, your voice on the telephone,
a little hoarse and quick
and full of New Jersey
sounds like the way a friend
describes mine: raspy, she says, and fast talking.
This morning when I call you
on my fortieth birthday,
I hear us together, drinking coffee
and bitching about Pop.
He's cranky, you say. I ask,
more than usual? He's out
when I call, so you talk freely,
and I miss the mornings
we'd pass in the kitchen.
The sound of your voice
floats through my dreams
and when I wake today, Mamma,
I am using it.
This is one of the things
I like about getting older:
the way I am more like you,
or my memory of you,
with every year I gather.
They seem to come faster now.
Between us, a hundred and four years
make a vee in the sky,
a migration of birds soaring
to a place we have been, and will
return to. Today I light a candle
and make the wish: where ever we land,
may we find a little kitchen,
brew some coffee, and lend the blue echo
of our voices, matched at last,
to all the birds still singing.

9-9-87: Forty-Two

At least I slept last night.
Up at 6 a.m., house quiet
cats are out, lover sleeping

Feels good to be up
alone in the kitchen
my family all safe.

Maybe this year can be
a feeling of home and settled
but still... the excitement outside

In eight years I will be fifty.

Change Is Silver

Change is silver.
It comes in the window at night
as the full moon wanes
and I am alone,
quiet, full of my own thoughts
and feelings.

This is the year
of wanting
to run away.

1990

Forty-Fourth Birthday in Boston

At a new lover's house
first time in twelve years
without the first love

I feel either fine
or quite remote,
not sure which.

Both lovers
recede from me
as does much else

my work, my poems,
myself, yet I am not
at all unhappy.

So I begin this birthday year
wondering and dreaming of what?

1991

Happy Birthday to Me

I am forty
I am still alive
and fights break out too early

(Two lovers are hard to please)

How we twirl time time time
pulling threads up from the blankets
in summer

Or now just before fall
already trees grow old
and red and full of death

Though they love to be alive.

1992

Happy Go Luck Me

Here I am at forty-six
with friends in Truro
watching gulls right here
on the bay

Old, older, olding.
Older than before.
Foghorn, gull calls,

waves mosey their way to shore.
Luck, love, loss,
less afraid of being alone

heading toward crone age, cronage
In my cronage time I will sing
to my solitude

To my mother, to the not-mother
and my mother laughing.
I can laugh and laugh and laugh

Sprout little hairs on my chin,
say what the hell and
turn my eyes toward heaven.

1993

Telescope

I look through the telescope
my cupped hand makes
and I see

Pines all shiny with rain
Still thick with green
pine, maple, oak

Right out my window
where I fall with love,
the happiness it brings

just to see time
in its changes, the moods
trees evoke just by living

So much sings!
Wind, bird, plane
and silvery rain

falling lightly after storm
What comfort it brings
what hope, what tenderness.

1994

So We Are Mortal

So we are mortal
so we want the touch
of fruit in our mouths
or wine.

So we need to feel honored,
proud, silly, sad, enraged,
disappointed, and love

lost, or losing. The way
that memory shifts and floats,
vanishing from the beginning of life.

I am forty-eight. So Mamma bought me
a cake with pink roses
and we drank sambuca all night long
with Aunt Jo.

1995

Aunt Jo

With a shot of whiskey
and a bowling ball
A brassy voice and a fierce fierce
mouth   the one they say I follow

You showed me
love inside argument
The fieriness
of belief
and how to share
a Hershey bar with almonds
a steak sandwich
a sapphire
one September

Birds Remembering

They do not use the stairs, the spirits of your ancestors.
—Diane diPrima, *The Calculus of Variation*

1. Bird of Sorrow

They don't fly in the window either, bad luck
that could bring. They don't come down
the chimney, no fluttering wings of birds
gone mad or astray. Sometimes though they come
out of my belly button, they cluster along
the slope of my shoulders, they roll right off
the tip of my tongue, after a slow crawl
through desire and fear. They remember
wild hands that strangled a song in my throat.
I floated like a movie star to another angle
to see if what I knew was happening. I lost
an earring, the wail in my mouth. I heard
the way my father's lips sneaked up above
his teeth, caressed the silver wings
of his partial plate, his too pink gums.
They made a zipper's hissing sound.
I was afraid. I had terrified hands, I
was sorrowful. Over his shoulder I noticed
the kitchen table was not clean.

2. Bird of Silence

It's great when the ancestors visit.
But when I try to take them into a crowd
they lose me, they leave me there, their
small voices become a low whisper. So
I can get to screaming with rage,
not meaning to. Not rage. It's more
desperate, urgent with light.

Some of the white girls tell me to shove it.
The class girls, you know what I mean. I say
shove it, really, they say lower your voice,
their pale hands measuring the air
like they own it. They're no blood relation
to me, my mother once said about my father,
and his side, the Sicilians. She was driving.
She screamed with rage unfamiliar to us both.
Her fist pounded and pounded the steering wheel,
she blazed with her anger. I lost her, I knew it.
To die for, I say some days, of the memories.

3. Silly Bird, I Love You

You're my favorite. Better than
the ponies of dreaming, you fly
up unexpected. What I love best
is your wild mouth, the way songs
come of your throat all cockeyed
and toothless. I'm laughing now.
Remember the way we love water?
It's mostly at seashore or lakeside
you find me. The rest of the time
it's a memory I long for. Little bird,
favorite bird, silly bird, I'm listening
in the sorrow and rage, in the madness
all purple, even your small songs
are lovely. Early this morning
you began to hum in my ear, a lover's
tongue, my throat starts to quiver
and then I'm singing.

4. Hot Bird of Longing

Ooh, I said

you just gave me a little sexual thrill
and oops I went hot through the middle
of lust again. It was morning near
the sea, early for unusual lust. I love
losing in moments of bliss, even alone.
Up the throat roams desire, the sea
is so large. You say you remember
once loving the dress that I wore,
the last time we danced all alone
in the woods. You called me dear.
Once you leaped over the bar
in your tux shirt, hot butch that you are,
and desire swam through me for hours.
Once you held lemons and limes
in the olive-skinned bowl of your hands,
long fingers caressing them whole, lovely,
you loved how I wanted you so easy,
dark eyes, gold chains round your neck
all shiny. I call you, recall you.

5. Crying Bird

Even the birds cry, Mamma.
Across species I hear the same old longing:
Come home, come home, this is our life,
oh Mamma, oh baby. I remember coarse
whispers rising in the night to see
you crying in the kitchen, back door
open to stars, the sound of the car,
leaving. By ourselves, Mamma, we could
have made it, it's still what I long for
alone in my forties. Not a child, but
to be yours again, the old ways we danced,
your palm tender on my cheek, the small
phrases you'd whisper, our secrets. Too
many years without you have made me come
loose from your treasure. Out here
on the sea I recall it and weep. I
think I've gone hard, Mamma, tough bird
in salt air. I think I've grown old,
Mamma, old to our longing. I'm rocking
and swaying in storm. I open my palms,
my mouth, welcoming the rain. I sing
a small song, it's full of blue air,
the same as our sorrow, what's left us
behind. If I return to my longing
what I might find is an infant of sorrow,
departure or, worse, left loose in the sea,
all alone, full of rage.

6. Bird of the Lake

Even in paradise small birds are homeless.
Over tea at the lake one fell from a tree
squawking with rage. It could have been
sorrow, desperate, madness. I fled back
and away from its rage, a mother offered
her finger till it landed and stayed,
its beak pointy, glaring. I
was afraid of its yelling, the blaze
in its eyes. Disease, I thought,
or dying. They're coming in waves.

Get real. A bird fell outada fuckin' tree.
That's it. So make a big deal of it,
be a poet again, go preen your feathers
in front of the angels. Ha Ha.
He says. The voice of his memory says.

My ancestors' wings belong to their shoulders,
angels of demons prance around, ridiculous.
They won't use the time, Sicilians, Calabrians,
wiseguys and hardheads. Stubborn, they lug
their burdens around for years.

'They were poor,' a white man said once, sure
of himself, grinning. They had no clothes.
They were dirty, they plunged their dirty
hands right into the bowls of spaghetti
set out on the table and ate, using
the raggedy skirts of the women to wipe
red sauce from their mouths

They are some of the women who tell me
to say so, but mostly in dreams: a bowl
of time full of rivers and sky. If
I try to stay quiet, I ache so, low
in my back or the center of longing.

Their voices yell below my heart.
'Pay attention to us,' they are screaming.
We love you.

Birthday, 1996

Forty-Nine

I wake solitary
full of the joy
of what's outside the window.
Slight rain.
Birds sing.
It's warm and the cats are near me.

What I love:
poems, house, cats, silence, rain
ocean, Mamma, friends, books.
Mowing the lawn. A tomato.
Freedom. Discipline. Practice.
Spirit. Dreams.

What I want: exactly the same.
(This came as a soft surprise.)
Add health with recent worries.

All along the years of time,
a bird may call, a bell may chime:
I am here I am here I am here

The familiar window as seasons change.
Who drops from view and who remains.
Who dances past the windowpane.

This year barrels along to fifty.
I want to be quiet and happy
and mostly alone.

Birthday Poem at Fifty

Sorrows out, poems in.
I can play with a fin to win
in the alleys. Always wondering
over the shoulder of time.
Bend after bend. Circle and arc
or ark. To go sailing, rise
up on a wave of time. Fling fifty
arms and screams toward sky.
Fly if you can. Fly. Fifty times
at least you've risen.

And more and more. Sorrows in.
Poems out. Try a grin
at zero. Start again. It's yours,
like an engine with a growl,
a purr, the time to prowl.

1997

At Fifty-One

Piece by piece the elderly apple tree out back
gives up an arm, a limb, a great branch
where a tire used to swing, where the cats,
when kittens and full of joy, climbed up and down
and even once one swung by his front paws,
clinging to the bough until rescued.

Branch and leaf and memory.
The day before my birthday.
I contemplate, self-consciously,
aging. Not afraid to show my sentiment,
my foolishness, my hope.

Friends have gone too, my arms emptier
this narrowing decade. Parents waver
on the edge of life, and I... I celebrate
being alive.

1998

Wren House

The wrens find the blue wren house, new
and proud on the post you repaired.
How do they know, you mused, like
an old poem, which way to go.

Cellular motion is all instinct,
action just out of conscious range.
Still, it's what fills the blood stream,
every single second we're alive:
loop and dive and eventual slide

into this: wistful lucky morning,
wrens finding home. My voice
alone inside the poem. How I enter
the center of life—through body
and already becoming the air
I am breathing.

2000

Camp Paradise

My fifty-fourth birthday in paradise.
I build a big fire to welcome me,
celebrate being alive,
full of confusion and insight.
Years of life,
running in the rain of childhood,
full of hope and expectation.
I was brave then, peddling my bike
racing away from fear and anger.
Then off to the love years of high school,
sweet and sexy and secretive.
And Oh, the bolder, unexpected, exhilarating
years since becoming woman.

All that I know is love and loss and memory.
A little luck. To see mist rising from the lake,
Lover inside and safe

and I am suddenly crying, like the loons,
across the whole damn lake, the whole damn lake
of being alive.

2001

Fifty-Four Again

What kind of bird is that, squawking its mind
loud, persistent, in love with the sound?

It is me, she sings, calling from the bill
of loon, skimming the surface, hungry.

And me. Wind that calls, 'fall, fall.'
reddening the leaves with age and wonder.

2001

Poem For My Birthday

Swim. Or fire. Which yields the chance for pleasure,
which for fear. Which might caress me, softly
alluring, or warm me to a heat I've
never known.

Last of summer. Last fire, last chance to swim,
last night's storm still hisses from the logs,
whisper or sinister, like church, sisters
hushing laughter of we girls, while Mary's

blue serenity looked at us with love,
welcoming as this fire, or lake beneath
clay dunes. An ear opens wide on a log
in the fire, and wind begins to pray:

'Hail Mary, full of morning, we all are like
thee. Blessed are we among trees, blessed
are the saplings and geese of all species.
Holy Mary, mother of all, sing for

our hopeful, now and all the hours we might know.'
It begins to be autumn, some leaves already
red. The storm has plumped the trees, the lake seems
satisfied, its gray-blue surface calmed by grey-blue sky.

I feel all my years shift well within me,
all their fires and lakes, and the wind,
the wind always hustling through the trees.

2002

Here I Am

Here I am at fifty-six
Before fifty-six I was young and full of hope
and at fifty-six I am still full of hope
but youth belongs to the past,
troubled and glorious.
The past was travelling through Europe
Woodstock
Anti-War Marches
living in Kenya
and all those years in North Jersey.

The past is a wonderful mother
and the lost brother I'll never stop grieving,
the father whose death set me free
yet now I miss him,
his roaming eye, his lopsided grin.

Now and always a poet,
if I were to have a gravestone
it would say only this:
She was a poet.

Once I was a daughter
a sister an aunt a cousin
a friend a nurse a wife
a teacher a not-mother a lover of women
and life and wine and tomatoes

Here I am.
Fifty-six.
A poet.

Stars in My Throat

A star blooms in my throat
my throat of love and sorrow
and its points, all five,
reach their fire into soft red folds
of throat and neck and time and hope

Star of wonder, star of joy,
star that misses a little boy
now gone to stars
now gone to flame
and my lonely star now sings
his name

2004

Love Poem after a Quarrel

And later still when hunger appears
on a Sunday afternoon, rain
falling softly in September, I lay
my mouth to yours, and wonder how love
comes to be after quarrels, and why
we argue as though we despise our lives
and yet as hours pass we reconcile
without cruel words to mark the air,
only touch again recalls what is there,
besides the mysteries, beneath the fire,
and later still, alongside our desire.

2005

Prose Birthday

I turned fifty-nine. Turned, a word that changes me. I turn into this year alone: without Mamma feels alone, like a sailboat surrounded by sea. There's a strength to it, even a small excitement that lives right alongside the fear, the grief, the loneliness.

Becoming elder, like my poem, then becomes alone and elder. A tree now perhaps, standing in full power, surrounded by other elders here and risen, and by saplings we might tend. I pray for a door to walk through, into the place I may be all of me, poems and service, and most of all love.

Her voice, wisdom and sweet peaches. Her gentle guiding, quiet and perceptive, hopeful. Sometimes, Mamma, your face emerges in front of me, photo or memory. I put my arms around you, and so too around me.

2006

Becoming Elder

When you have no more uncles
to lean on or cook with or argue with
at holiday meals, no more *commari*,
no aunts, no feisty old women telling you
what to guard against, what to watch out for,
what to do with your men, your women, your kids,
your sauce, your life, your soul, your heart

No more stuffed artichokes, no *braciole* the way
Mamma made it, no more obligatory visits
to the tables of love and fury, no more kids who'll
remember a thing you know, no more language
in gesture of shoulder or chin, no more laughter,
no smoke, no poker games, no macaroni, no gravy,
no ricotta pie, no more wounded hearts, no secrets
tumbling like fists pummeling the air, no more sobs
long stranded in throats bulging with rage and love,
with disappointment, with pride, no more rich, raspy
cigarette voices, no one to blame, no one to praise,
no one to see, no one to know how old you've become,
or how you've failed or succeed, no one to tell
how much you miss what you swore you would forget.

2006

God's Door

This year on my birthday
I push open God's door. Softly,
and with some fear.

2006

My Birthday Poem

Begun in fear and prayer
Surrounded by love and friends
The body's tenderness soldiers on
Embraces fear
Full of Faith
Full of Beauty
(the sunflower's brave head,
a handful of basil from our garden)
marching right along side
our fragile mortal selves
our endless souls
our blessed journey.

2007

Everyday Faith

It would seem the cat is oblivious
to death, or the fear of all death means.
Perhaps death is the opposite of faith.
The cat sits in the windowsill, a late
summer day. We've just come home
with two weeks worth of groceries.
Cancer free, the doctor said, his neat
white quiet head tucking down, gentle,
sincere. You found a surgeon much like you.
Quiet. Intense as the scalpel in his hand, the faith
in yours. Gentle. Sincere. And so afraid,
or is that me who fears, or all of our fears,
except for the faithful cat who washes her paws
in afternoon light as she always does. We
stretch out on our bed near the window
for an afternoon which has an everyday feeling
we will begin to practice.

2007

At Sixty-One: Gratitude

Gentle rain, small thunder,
and me, at sixty-one. Blue door
open at last and the Spirit
has a home inside my chest,
heart and soul, body and mind
and what a surprise, what
great joy to find love
embracing me.

2008

Poem at Sixty-Two

At sixty-two, moments pass as fast
as images in glass.
Once so young I couldn't even see
my own face reflected, or the times
that would someday trace it in lines

I wake at sixty-two praying for grace,
and to recall all that's come before,
memories in songs of birds and Beatles,
scrapbooks full of romance and travel
and the long heat of being alive.

My tender self, growing old, ever more
vulnerable to my heartbeat.

Again at Sixty-Two

in the language of the mystics, God is my me . . .
—Lectio

It's late. It's hot. And the God-door inside
me has shut down for the night.
Still, I sit here, pry it open with my pen,
with my fingernails,
with my frustrated fists I pound and pound.
Silence and silence and silence.

Night sky keeps stars in closed up clouds.
I can't hear the voices of heaven singing.
Sleep is rumbling its necessary call
and I begin to fall, spent, into its arms.
It is then I see the God I've been seeking,
the me-God, the God-me, the sleepy, patient,
humble one waiting for me to know me.
In that marriage of spirits, I dive deep
into a long and graceful sleep.

9 September 2010

Crying my way to sixty-three, plenty of tears
in my rivers of sorrow and bliss. Blessed
to be here among trees, the pronoun *we*,
the sky full of God. All the mighty tangles
and snares, fears of illness and of health,
of the life still before me. Yet a woman I've loved
is leaving and I'd like a bit of respite from the world.

The poem moves
through cell and blood stream,
desire, body, spirit, like a good rain storm
clearing away what needs to be cleared.

And then there is peace, another word
for love, another word for being alive,
another word for laughter.

Purple Portrait of a Stranger at Long Nook

I love your purples against the sea,
the sweet violet of you as you bend
for shell and stone, the erotic purple circle
of your soft skirt raised up by purple wind
and the sea behind you dark as a purpled bruise
at the wave's crest, the soft pink of your naked feet
against rain-tanned sand, the purple silence
between each wave where I see you,
violet sweet, bending at the waist, spinning purple circles.

Long Nook, Truro, Ma.
22 August 2010

Sixty-Four

Who knows what faith means inside
the body of love. Who know what
love means, inside the body of faith.
Chalice. Tabernacle. Eucharist.
Peaches in sunlight. A woman's
kiss, her yielding lips. I dip
my fingers in the holy water of love.

Or is it Faith? Or human bliss?
Body my star, my river, my breath:
I come undone by faith and love.
Still I believe I see the trees
lifted by dreams on their way to stars.

2011

Birthday at Sixty-Five

Another door: its opening holds history,
its future spins like my globe of childhood.
Long ago stories float, dreamlike.
I am blessed in this golden present:
a double rainbow after my birthday storm
stretches itself across the sky.
And then my mother's face returns
as the sun, her brimming eyes, her trembling
hands, our entwined journeys.

Now it is me. Here,
as I saw myself thirty-five years ago—at a desk,
before a window, always gazing through the trees,
hair gone gray, days I only think and pray.
I can begin to let old sorrows drift away.
I open my hands in moonlight where mysteries live,
the sacred and the scary, shiny, present
as stars that fill our sky, alive and dying, like me,
like my body of love.

Poem at Sixty-Six

Seagulls.
Herring Cove.

If I learn how to sing
what bird might welcome me?
What wind will lift feathered wings,
to what sky, afloat with what souls?
What souls are we who drift
amidst our lives?

2013

Birthday Poem at Sixty-Seven

With friends at the ocean,
fall wind blowing in, sky pink with itself,
the bliss of being alive. I record the waves
thinking of *Il Postino* and his love of Neruda.
What notes I play or write can never reach
the pure beauty of waves. God's voice
is a mirror of sea, the thrill of new birds
calling. Surrounded by love, by the ocean
we watched the sun rise at Long Nook,
saw the bluies leap and shine in dark blue waves
at dawn. When dolphins came by flashing their humanity,
I saw us all coasting to oblivion, heard dolphin calls
melancholy and euphoric.

Divorce Poem

For Mother Goose

In a nursery rhyme, the dish
runs away with the spoon: a love story
about two women. The dish,
a frilled beauty. The spoon wifely rounded.
Each had her own menu.

One day, the spoon came down
too hard on the dish. The tiniest
crack settled in. The spoon had begun
to have enough. The dish preened
in the silvery glow of the toaster,
smoothing butter into the tiny crack.
Dish was vain and spoon always wanted
to be filled, then spill over into dish.

You can see both had the habit of egotism,
a fancy word not in the nursery rhyme.
But here it is, overflowing the spoon,
heaped up on the dish.

They both hear the little dogs laugh,
the fiddle still playing with the cat. The moon,
that last romantic, echoes the lowing cows.
Of course, the dish and the spoon run away again,
sneaking out of the place setting with someone new.
Dish to dish and spoon to spoon? I'll leave that
to you, Mother Goose, and the waning moon.

2015

A Tulip's Story

The last red tulip cleaves to the bowl,
clear glass, her red tears dripping, her weak neck
heading nowhere but down. I who put her there
want only to watch. All year I have flagged
and surged, tucked into this body aging fast
beyond its wisdom.

I still dream of love and romance, and glad
though I am that I do, it's remote as Snow White's story.
But the tulip is real and alive and may remember
when, bulb like, she nestled underground
throughout the long winter, covered in white
snow, her red hope waiting.

2015

Iris

Remember this: I love yellow iris,
companion to deep purple,
both on my table. Opposite
beauties, they lean toward each other,
as though sharing a secret desire.

Their petals are memories:
once the garden was home. Once
we were alive. Once we quoted
Roethke all steamed up in his father's
greenhouse. Now, here we are,
still life, resting on green strands of memory.

Potato

Mama Potato comes out of the hot August earth
with a lip turned up and nose held high. Her eye
is most alive—fierce, fiery with wisdom of her stage.
Unwavering, glittery, like a star burning out memories
of blight and what some only hungered for—
her creaminess, her crisp edges hot and sharp
when heated high. Salt lick of skin along
potato's rim, the tongue's desire
tucked in, for now.

She huddles with her spuds, four, bumpy
and round. Her chin sprouts grizzly hairs,
like mine. We are in our cronage, though
her roundly figure and billowing middle
keep something young about her.

Maybe she's just past her prime,
too fleshy, too soft in spots, achy
around her rigid neck. Tired.
So she will nurture but not-mother,
a difference as small as the sharpening eye
or the root of the tongue, or a potato,
lost too long underground.

2015

Tomatoes

The tomatoes too are full of stories,
splitting their red seams in a rush,
a frenzy. Time vanishes so fast when seeds
return to earth, garden a bed of wonder for the last
and the first. First, pride takes over. Flowers
preen in sunlight. Even at six, Sian saw them:
'They're beautiful!' He raised his arms up,
in praise, a word that comes from prayer,
which is like a seed

tucked away in the richness of heart, the muscle
that matters most, behind a cage of bones.
All life long secrets whisper from them, almost
discernible, though it is not words that shape the darkness.
Or the light. Or the mysteries. How I became who I am
begins with stars that God made. We know them
as heartbeats in the terrible sky,
where sun and moon have their reasons.
Everything does. This pen. The still ticking clock,
the memory of women making sauce from ripe tomatoes.

2015

Summer Solstice, 2016

So I'm looking through the skylight
at the solstice moon. In a view of stars
and darkening clouds the moon's full
majesty is found. In it, I float toward
gratitude, grace, the great love.

Too, there's this giant sized branch of an oak
hovering just above the skylight. Moon's
light is sinuous, slipping in between
smaller branches and the fingers of leaves,
the big branch sways, seductive.

Later, two plump bluebirds near the tree house
are singing.

Birthday Poem at Sixty-Nine

The measured way in which she walks
uneasy on stones, then sways into
flowers purpling the sky.

This is myself, an image of aging.
Summer has just begun to turn.
The old box elder, long gone,
reminds me. Once, I saw its leaves turn red,
early August, a month of sorrows. I was not yet
menopausal, though I sensed it. Some
one died. Some one left. There never was
an infant, except me, another time.

I have weeds in my heart, a friend once said,
they keep me from loving. There are stones too,
that may hurt while praying, or measuring
steps while walking home.

Approaching Seventy

Body begins her sweet decay
bone by bone, day by day,

pulling close to an earthier place.
Ears fail. Eyes fade.

No sorrow grips her heart. That's strange.
We imagined grief at the nearing days.
More playful with life's rhymes,

I float. I spin. I am on time.

Body still sings our song,
as it has. All along. All along.

Shadows at Seventy-One

The shadow of my old dog
passes through the archway,
her golden fur as sleek and shiny
as when she was a long ago puppy.

My youth has passed through
the same archway. Hundreds
of paces forward and back,
to now. I stand still and listen:

Who calls from sky
Who waves from sea
Who used to be used to be
used to be me.

Mornings: At Seventy-Two

1

Fire burst out of my ear,
and thousands of particles of light
lit up the room with a bluish glow.

I let go of thinking what I knew.
It wasn't you after all, but truth
hid in the bedsheets damp with imagined love.

I don't know the meaning of fire,
or light either. I know I pray
through the skylights when trees

are waving and green. I know
I love that and the quiet
settling in after grief.

2

If I write left-handed
will my dreams come true?
Will my right brain be happier,
more at home, more in love
with ideas?

Will I dance ever again
in the kitchen with Mamma
laughing and smoking while red sauce bubbles?
Will I know I wrote this poem
when I am eighty or before?

My arm's in a sling, my wing. My right hand woman
scribbles in the stars, scratches at the blue door
like the cats, jumping into morning sky

Warning: At Seventy-Three

While I was away, the old pine tree
fell, so elegantly. Her vulnerable thigh
came to rest on the redwood deck, her
neck sheared off further on down. But
she spread her obligingly,
though wind, they day, was high,
she damaged neither chipmunk nor chair,

nor air, which put her there.
Her attitude hurts me. So womanly
her posture, tilting careful even in loss,
like a woman afraid to sing
or to wish on the stars.

What's left of her arms she brings in,
hugging herself in the first real cold
of the year. She's a tangle of skinny limbs
and leftover brown and crumpled leaves
that settle there, like Medusa's hair.

At Seventy-Four

The neck goes first,
wrinkly underneath
the chin, and then
it all lets loose
in a cry of love:
Good body, 'my horse,
my hound.' I find
you alive with memories
and ancient love stories,
the heartbreak of loss
mother father sister brother
stars in my eyes
the spin and whirl of spring
the long bloom of winters.

Here I go, leaping into
the last quarter and then
my ashes will fly to bliss.

Seventy-Five: Today

In memory of Pat and Deborah Sorrentino

I'm full of grief for everything these days:
lost flowers crowded into garden or vase,
the garden all big weeds and lazy seeds
and neglect laces my eyes with tears.
Like the river merchant's wife, I'm in love
with what's missing: youth, passion, laughter
and hope, despairing the present.
The butterflies' remarkable colors,
their swaying wings hum in the changing air,
flitting from the last places you were: Home,
the road you took to my house, or the doctor
who let you go too soon. Another minute,
a red light, a last minute ice cream, or
a look at the lake beneath the sun.

I stop there, before I get to the spot I pass
almost every day where he tore into you,
unknown, just driving home.
We hold you now, so vibrant in our loss.
And we, enriched and bereft, do what will
only be done: we hold you close,
we let you free.

About the Author

Rachel Guido deVries is a poet and fiction writer. *The Birthday Years* is her fifth collection of poems. Her novel, *Tender Warriors,* was published by Firebrand Books in 1986. Until recently she was a poet in the public schools for thirty years. She directed the Feminist Writers' Workshop at Wells College in the 1980s, and founded and directed the Community Writers Project in the 1990s. She lives in Cazenovia, New York, with her two cats, Angelo and Fredo.

VIA Folios

A refereed book series dedicated to the culture of Italians and Italian Americans.

GIL FAGIANI. *Chianti in Connecticut*. Vol 63. Poetry.

BASSETTI & D'ACQUINO. *Italic Lessons*. Vol 62. Italian/American Studies.

CAVALIERI & PASCARELLI, Eds. *The Poet's Cookbook*. Vol 61. Poetry/Recipes.

EMANUEL DI PASQUALE. *Siciliana*. Vol 60. Poetry.

NATALIA COSTA, Ed. *Bufalini*. Vol 59. Poetry.

RICHARD VETERE. *Baroque*. Vol 58. Fiction.

LEWIS TURCO. *La Famiglia/The Family*. Vol 57. Memoir.

NICK JAMES MILETI. *The Unscrupulous*. Vol 56. Humanities.

BASSETTI. ACCOLLA. D'AQUINO. *Italici: An Encounter with Piero Bassetti*.
    Vol 55. Italian Studies.

GIOSE RIMANELLI. *The Three-legged One*. Vol 54. Fiction.

CHARLES KLOPP. *Bele Antiche Stòrie*. Vol 53. Criticism.

JOSEPH RICAPITO. *Second Wave*. Vol 52. Poetry.

GARY MORMINO. *Italians in Florida*. Vol 51. History.

GIANFRANCO ANGELUCCI. *Federico F.* Vol 50. Fiction.

ANTHONY VALERIO. *The Little Sailor*. Vol 49. Memoir.

ROSS TALARICO. *The Reptilian Interludes*. Vol 48. Poetry.

RACHEL GUIDO DE VRIES. *Teeny Tiny Tino's Fishing Story*.
    Vol 47. Children's Literature.

EMANUEL DI PASQUALE. *Writing Anew*. Vol 46. Poetry.

MARIA FAMÀ. *Looking For Cover*. Vol 45. Poetry.

ANTHONY VALERIO. *Toni Cade Bambara's One Sicilian Night*. Vol 44. Poetry.

EMANUEL CARNEVALI. *Furnished Rooms*. Vol 43. Poetry.

BRENT ADKINS. et al., Ed. *Shifting Borders. Negotiating Places*. Vol 42. Conference.

GEORGE GUIDA. *Low Italian*. Vol 41. Poetry.

GARDAPHÈ, GIORDANO, TAMBURRI. *Introducing Italian Americana*.
    Vol 40. Italian/American Studies.

DANIELA GIOSEFFI. *Blood Autumn/Autunno di sangue*. Vol 39. Poetry.

FRED MISURELLA. *Lies to Live By*. Vol 38. Stories.

STEVEN BELLUSCIO. *Constructing a Bibliography*. Vol 37. Italian Americana.

ANTHONY JULIAN TAMBURRI, Ed. *Italian Cultural Studies 2002*.
    Vol 36. Essays.

BEA TUSIANI. *con amore*. Vol 35. Memoir.

FLAVIA BRIZIO-SKOV, Ed. *Reconstructing Societies in the Aftermath of War*.
    Vol 34. History.

TAMBURRI. et al., Eds. *Italian Cultural Studies 2001*. Vol 33. Essays.

ELIZABETH G. MESSINA, Ed. *In Our Own Voices*.
    Vol 32. Italian/American Studies.

STANISLAO G. PUGLIESE. *Desperate Inscriptions*. Vol 31. History.

Milton Keynes UK
Ingram Content Group UK Ltd.
UKHW031041160924
448404UK00005B/431

9 781599 542218